Hysterical Historicals

Jeanne Willis

Illustrated by Spike Gerrell

Contents

WARNING! 3

Lawrence Nightingale 5

Julius Teaser 22

Percy Bysshe Smelley 40

The Wrong Brothers 56

Marco Pillow 76

WARNING!
This is not a normal history book

You've probably read lots of history books, so you know what to expect. You've learnt dates, facts and information about real people who lived in the past?

Well, I hope you're sitting down, because this history book is unlike anything you've read before. That's because almost none of it is true. You might have heard of Florence Nightingale, but I bet you've never heard of her brother Lawrence, have you? That's because he didn't exist. And neither did Julius Teaser, Percy Bysshe Smelley, Marco Pillow, or even the Wrong Brothers. Sorry about that, history would have been a whole lot funnier if they had.

At the start of each story there is a short introduction which gives you information about the real historical period when the story is set. The introductions also tell you about any real historical characters mentioned in the story. But apart from the introductions, there's hardly a true word in the whole book. Whatever you do, don't use it to help you do your history homework.

And if you do, don't say I didn't warn you ...

Lawrence Nightingale: Historical Background

Florence Nightingale was the heroic nurse who saved the lives of many sick and injured soldiers during the Crimean War. She is often called 'the founder of modern nursing'. She did many extraordinary things in her long life, but she never had a brother called Lawrence. Mind you, when you read the story you may feel that's just as well.

Florence was born in 1820. She came from a wealthy family and she had one sister, Frances Parthenope (Parthe for short). Her mother, father and sister were horrified when Florence decided to become a nurse because nursing was not a respectable profession for women at that time. But Florence was determined, so she trained to be a nurse in Germany. When she came back to England she helped to run the Hospital for Invalid Gentlewomen in London.

When the Crimean War broke out in 1854, there were many shocking newspaper reports about British soldiers dying because of hunger and sickness. They received very poor medical care in the battlefield hospitals. Florence longed to go out to the Crimea to help and she got her chance when her friend Sidney Herbert, who was Minister for War, asked her to lead a team of nurses working close to the Crimean battlefields.

When she got to the military hospital at Scutari, Florence was shocked by the horrific conditions in which the soldiers were living. The hospital was unhygienic and the food was horrible – it not only tasted disgusting, but often it was actually mouldy! No wonder so many soldiers were dying. Under Florence's command the hospital became cleaner, more hygienic and the food improved too. (She didn't invent penicillin, though, whatever the story might suggest!)

When Florence came back to Britain in 1856, she was a heroine. She continued to work hard to improve conditions in hospitals and in 1860 she started her own training school for nurses at St Thomas' Hospital in London. Throughout her life she kept working to improve hospitals and nursing, even writing letters to important people when she was lying ill in bed. In 1907 she became the first woman ever to be awarded the Order of Merit. She died at the age of 90, in 1910.

Did you know?

- Florence Nightingale was named after the city where she was born – Florence, in Italy. It's just as well she wasn't born in Bognor!
- Florence was a very serious person and she hated being famous. I wonder what she would have thought about the story that follows?

Lawrence Nightingale: The World's Worst Nurse

No doubt you have heard of Florence Nightingale, but in case you fell asleep during your history lesson at school, here's a quick reminder. She was the posh Victorian lass with the strict hair parting and lace cap who upset the toffs by doing something even more shocking than showing her ankles – she became a nurse.

You'd think her mother would have been delighted that she wasn't sitting on her bustle[1] all day sewing tapestry cushions in the parlour. But no! Old Mother Nightingale threw a hissy fit, fainted in the closet and had to have her corsets loosened by the maid.

[1] a frame or pad worn under a skirt to give it a full shape

Why? Because in the olden days, people thought it very unladylike to run around in a crinoline[2] carrying steaming bedpans in a ward full of sick, sweaty soldiers. Nice, rich girls didn't do that – only nasty, poor girls who couldn't find a husband.

'Florence, I insist that you give up this ridiculous idea of helping the sick and dying immediately!' wailed Mrs Nightingale, taking a short, sharp snort of smelling salts. 'It's frightfully selfish, not to mention embarrassing. If you go through with this, I will never be able to show my face at The Summer Ball for Anti-Feminist Gentlewomen ever again.'

'Keep your wig on, Mama,' said Florence. 'I'm off to the Crimea with thirty-eight assorted good women and you can't stop me.'

'Sounds like one heck of a hen party,' said her big sister, Frances. 'Can I come, Flo? I fancy a knees-up.'

'Put your parasol away, Fanny,' said Florence, grabbing her muffler and stuffing it into an ostrich skin suitcase. 'There's a war on. I'm off to Scutari Hospital to tend the wounded. The only *knees up* there will be bandaged and riddled with gangrene.'

---

[2] a rigid petticoat

'Eughh!' said Frances, gagging on a silver spoon full of lark's tongue porridge. 'That's so *gross*. Why can't you marry a nice baron, have twelve babies and die in childbirth like a normal woman?'

'Because,' said Florence, 'I want to go to Turkey and become the founder of modern nursing.'

'How will you get there, you silly girl?' said her Mother. 'They haven't invented the aeroplane yet. Now go and put your hair in ringlets. I've invited that lovely Mr Monkton Milnes round for tea and crumpets.'

But Florence had no intention of stuffing her face with carbs and becoming a bride. On 22 August 1854, she sailed across the Black Sea to Balaklava where the main British army camp was based.

However, when Florence arrived at Selimiye Barracks in Scutari with her gaggle of chums from medical college, nothing prepared her for the shocking sight she encountered – her useless younger brother disguised as a matron in charge of a tent full of injured troops.

'Hello, Sis!' he boomed. He'd always liked

dressing-up when he was a young boy and Florence saw straight through his disguise.

'Lawrence!' she shrieked. 'What the flibbertigibbet are *you* doing here and why are you wearing a frock? You told Papa you were on the front line fighting the pesky Russians.'

Lawrence adjusted his wig and pulled a face.

'Yes, well that was a bit of a fib.' He said. 'The front line isn't nearly as much fun as I thought. It's quite dangerous out there, Flo-Bo. I don't want to end up like these chaps. That fellow in the end bed had his entire head blown off by a cannon ball. I tried to stick it back on but he's gone very quiet. Sulking, probably.'

Florence swept the ward with her eyes. What it really needed was a good going-over with a broom, a mop and several gallons of disinfectant.

'This place is filthier than a chimney sweep's sock!' said Florence. 'It's bloodier than a butcher's braces. Where's the soap?' Lawrence looked at her as if she was mad.

'Soap?' he snorted. 'That is so like ... a *girl*. What the Dickens do we want soap for? We're blokes!' The stench was overwhelming. Florence pinched her nostrils together.

'Health ad hygiene,' she said. 'Cleadliness id bery imbordand!'

'Pardon?' said Lawrence. 'Since when did you

learn to speak Welsh?'

Florence let go of her nose and repeated herself clearly.

'Cleanliness is very important,' she said. 'Where there's dirt, there's germs and germs lead to infection.' Lawrence flicked a rat dropping off the hospital trolley.

'I can't see any germs,' he said.

'Duh! They're invisible to the naked eye,' said Florence. 'Ladies, roll up your mutton sleeves. Rip up your petticoats for cloths and bandages. I want this ward and these patients spotless by lunchtime.' Lawrence's eyes lit up.

'Lunch?' he said. 'Oh goody! Has Mummy sent a hamper? I haven't eaten since Tuesday and all I had then was a slice of dog meat in a bun full of weevils.'

'We're starving!' groaned the soldiers.

Florence took her brother to one side.

'These men will die if they do not get a decent meal inside them. Why is there no food in the pantry and nothing in the medicine cupboard?'

Lawrence folded his arms and stamped his foot.

'I am *not* walking to the grocers in the rain,' he said. 'The surgeon uses the pantry to store his golf clubs and there *is* something in the medicine cupboard, actually.'

'Only alcohol,' said Florence. 'I shall use it to sterilize the instruments.'

'Instruments?' said Lawrence. 'There's a band? How splendid! The entertainment here is rubbish.' Florence shook her head.

'Not musical instruments, *surgical* instruments.'

'You'll be lucky,' said Lawrence, blowing his nose on the only clean tea towel. 'We've run out. We've been having to make do with a penknife, a poker and a set of nut crackers.'

'Don't remind me!' screamed a young private.

If Florence had been born in this century she would have whipped out her mobile and sent an urgent text to the Prime Minister to send supplies immediately. Instead, she had to bribe a small boy and send him by mule to the nearest souk with a shopping list as long as a monkey's arm: nose pegs, dressings, boil ointment, toilet rolls, washing soda, donkey mince, Turkish delight, copy of *Nursing Times*, etc.

'Hurry back, and don't look in the basket, young man,' she said. 'Some of those items are personal.'

Unfortunately, the market was a long way away and the mule was stubborn. Before the boy had returned, the patients in Scutari caught a dreadful plague, the like of which the medical profession had never seen before. By the end of the week, the death rate was soaring.

'They're dropping like flies. I can't imagine why,' said Lawrence, batting away a swarm of bluebottles as another body was carted off to the burial pit.

'This is all your fault, Lolly!' snapped Florence. 'You really are the world's worst nurse. You couldn't dress a salad, let alone a bullet wound. This ward is an absolute dump. It's almost as bad as your bedroom at home. I'm telling Mama.'

If Florence hadn't pinned her plaits into funny doughnuts round her ears, Lawrence would have grabbed them and swung her round.

'Don't you dare tell Mama!' he shouted. 'If you do I'll ... I'll ... run your bloomers up the flagpole!' Suddenly, Florence gave a small yelp and crumpled to the floor.

'I never touched her, honest,' protested Lawrence.

'Lawks-a-mussy!' gasped a volunteer nurse called Ruby as she examined the throbbing pustules on Florence's chest. 'I do declare Miss Nightingale has gone down with that foul new disease. Hurry, Mr Lawrence, she needs rest and victuals or she may die!' Lawrence scratched his lousy head.

'Victuals? They sound like something out of a Dickens novel.'

'That's just my old-fashioned way of saying she needs food, sir.' said Ruby, 'I beseech you, search for some. Your beloved sister is fading fast.'

Lawrence did his sums. He had two siblings, but if Flo-Bo went belly up, he'd only have to share his inheritance with Fanny when Papa snuffed it. Should he go for the two-way split or the three-way split? It was a no-brainer.

'Flo will be fine. Stop fussing,' he said, polishing his dainty button boots with a horribly stained rag.

'I beg you, sir!' pleaded Ruby. 'Spare her a morsel. If she should pass away, there will be precious little achieved in the field of medicine by women this century.'

'So? You can't tell me what to do,' said Lawrence. 'I'm a gentleman.' Ruby looked him up and down and snorted.

'I shall tell your papa that you wear ladies' clothing.' Lawrence adjusted his lace gloves and stomped off towards the kitchen.

'Alright, alright. I'm going.'

Apart from a pile of assorted limbs and a dead crow there was nothing in the larder. He considered cooking the crow but as he didn't know how to light the stove, he gave up and went for a lie down.

As he dozed, he became aware of an interesting smell coming from below. It was then that he suddenly remembered the old plate of donkey curry he'd left under his hammock. He reached down and picked up the dish. It had been festering in the heat for three months and to his surprise it had grown an enormous, bright green Afro made from mould.

'Flo will never notice,' he told himself, licking his fingers. 'There's a nice scrap of meat here.'

He slid out of the hammock, hurried to his sister's bedside and pressed a spoonful of mouldy curry to her pale lips.

'Open wide, Sis. Here comes the steam train ... choo choo!'

Too weak to fight him off, she swallowed it. There is an old saying: 'What doesn't kill you makes you stronger.' In this instance, Florence Nightingale should have died of food poisoning. Instead, the opposite happened. Overnight, her fever went, her boils burst and to everyone's amazement, by the afternoon she was sitting up, laughing, joking and doing a bit of crochet.

'It's a miracle!' cried Ruby.

Miracle or not, it was a major medical breakthrough. Being a clever old stick, Florence realized that the mould on the rotten meat must have acted like a shot of penicillin and destroyed the disease. So, as soon as the boy came back with the shopping, she cooked up a curry, cultivated some more spores and gave them to her suffering patients. The survival rate shot up. By the end of the war, the disease with no name was wiped out.

Teachers might tell you that this was all down to Florence Nightingale and her amazing nursing skills. But if a certain younger brother hadn't left his dirty dish under his bed, there would have been no cure. His laziness and hatred of washing-up saved hundreds of lives. Possibly thousands. Remind your mother of this the next time she moans because you haven't brought your plate down.

There is no mention of Lawrence Nightingale in the history books. But he does get a mention in an ancient medical dictionary in the Turkish library. Look under 'L' and you'll find him there, written in Latin:

Lurgii disgusticae Lawrencia

In other words, Lawrence's Lurgy. The symptoms are far too disturbing to list here, but credit where credit's due, not many people can boast that they have a disease named after them. We salute you, Lawrence.

Papa would be proud.

Julius Teaser: Historical Background

You won't be surprised to find out that there never really was a Roman Emperor called Julius Teaser! Julius Caesar, on the other hand, definitely existed. He was a Roman politician and general, and his main claim to fame was that he seized power and made himself dictator of Rome – eventually paving the way for the first Roman Emperor, his nephew Augustus.

Julius Caesar was born into a powerful Roman family. He was a clever and ambitious young man and quickly made a name for himself in Roman politics. He got one important political job after another, eventually becoming governor of a Roman province called Gaul.

During Julius' time as governor he conquered the whole of the area that is now France and Belgium. He was famous for his skill as a general. He even invaded Britain twice (in 55 and 54 BCE).

When he returned to Rome, however, Julius lost no time in annoying the Senate which governed the city. He refused to accept the Senate's authority, which led to a civil war. During the war, Julius and his allies fought against the Roman Republic. Julius won the war and went on to make himself consul and dictator. Dictatorship was always meant to be a temporary thing, for use in times of crisis only, but in 44 BCE Julius made himself dictator for life. The remaining republican senators were horrified and decided that they had to get rid of Julius. So, in March 44 BCE, he was assassinated by a group of senators. This led to another round of civil wars which finally brought about the end of the Roman Republic and the arrival of Augustus, the first Roman Emperor.

Roman circuses

The story of Julius Teaser may not have much to do with the historical Julius Caesar, but Julius Teaser's amazing shows in the story are based on historical fact. The Romans loved gladiatorial fights in which humans battled to the death, or fought with wild animals such as lions. Huge amphitheatres like the Colosseum in Rome were used to stage wild animal shows as well as fights. Sometimes the amphitheatres were even flooded to recreate massive sea battles!

Plebs and patricians

At many times in history, there was a big gap between the rich and the poor in Roman society. Much of the power was in the hands of a small group of families, known as patricians. Meanwhile, the ordinary people of Rome, known as the plebeians or plebs, had very little power.

Did you know?

- Roman gladiators were mostly slaves, prisoners of war or condemned criminals. Most of them were men, but there were a few female gladiators!
- Roman games were brutal. At the opening games at the Colosseum in Rome, over 9,000 wild animals were killed.

Julius Teaser: The World's Worst Prankster

Nero   Caligula   Commodus   Julius Teaser

It is a well-known fact that Ancient Rome had more than its fair share of mad emperors. Nero was nuts in a nasty way. He cut off his first wife's head, showed it to his girlfriend and also killed his own mum. What a charmer!

Then there was Caligula, who had long conversations with the moon and made his horse a senator. Commodus was a power freak. He named everything after himself and liked to dress up in a bearskin loincloth and insist that his subjects call him Hercules. Goodness knows what they called him behind his back.

But there was another crazy emperor that the history books fail to mention – he was just too silly for words. His name? It was Julius Teaser. Born on April Fool's Day in 80 BCE, he was the only son of Sillius Maximus and Luna Twiticus.

Having a clown for a father, Julius should have grown up in a jolly household, but his mother had a very short temper. And it was no wonder – it was hard enough living with a husband who kept gluing her sandals to the floor as a joke, let alone looking after a baby who did disgusting tricks with his dummy. Unable to cope, she abandoned Julius in the forest where he was brought up by hyenas. It showed. He had the most awful giggle.

At the age of two he was found and adopted by the widowed Empress Lacrimosa who was desperate for a child, even if it was barking. Julius had everything a small boy could wish for – a grand villa, lark's tongues for tea and his very own slave. It should have been a happy childhood, but the Empress was a misery. She wept and wailed and gnashed her teeth from morning to night and had no sense of humour at all.

Missing the comforting cackle of his hyena mother, Julius tried everything to make Lacrimosa laugh: he pulled funny faces, he did silly walks. He even made himself a false nose out of a tomato, but nothing made her smile.

It seemed as if Julius was doomed to a life of gloom, but one autumn he made a breakthrough. He was in the garden riding his toy chariot when he came across a bucket of rosehips picked by the slaves. Wondering if they were good to eat, he bit into one, only to find that it was full of fluffy bits which made him itch – these fluffy bits became the seeds of a brilliant idea. Wearing leather gauntlets to protect his hands, he split some open and collected the itchy rosehip seeds in his hanky.

The King of Egypt was visiting the Empress for a few days. He was a pompous oaf and, knowing that his mother hated the King, Julius thought he'd make the perfect victim. One night, as the King slept, he crept into the guest room and, seeing the royal toga folded on the chair, he tipped the seeds into it and slipped away.

By the time the King came down for breakfast, he was itching terribly, but he had no idea why. It was all he could do not to scratch at the table. By the time he'd eaten his eggs, he was fidgeting and squirming and pulling such strange faces that even the Empress was amused. She couldn't stop giggling. By the third course, the itching had driven the King insane and with a howl of frustration he flung his toga off and jumped into the fountain.

Empress Lacrimosa laughed hysterically – just like a hyena. It was music to Julius' ears, and now that he knew what tickled her funny bone he became a full-time practical joker. He suspended a flour sack over a Roman arch and was delighted to see his mother crease up when it spilled over the poor, unsuspecting soldiers. Encouraged, he glued coins to the cobbles and clutched his sides as he watched the plebeians trying to pick them up. He put a baby crocodile in the toilet and he even switched the signs at the public baths so that the ladies went into the men's pool by mistake. And once smelt, his stink bombs were never forgotten.

Julius Teaser never grew out of being a prankster. In fact, he got much worse with age. His mother eventually died from laughing, but even when he became Emperor, no one was safe from his practical jokes.

He loved to hold feasts so he could fool his dinner guests. He began by loosening the legs on the chairs so that they collapsed under the weight of the diners. He glued the wine goblets to the table, swapped the salt for sugar and served fruit made of wax.

The fun didn't stop there, though. Many of his distinguished guests had travelled a long way to visit him and had to stay for the night. After an evening spent falling off furniture and choking on fake food, they couldn't wait to go to bed, only to find that Julius had arranged the sheets so they couldn't get their feet in. Or had filled the room with bees. Or had pinched their right-foot sandals.

Julius just couldn't help himself. If he held a chariot race at the Hippodrome, he always changed someone's round wheels for square ones. Or he'd grease the seat so the driver slid out. Or let a rhinoceros loose in the crowd.

'I wish my darling Mater was here to see this!' he'd shriek as the rhino tossed the competitors into the audience. 'She would see the funny side.'

Other people didn't find him quite so funny, but because Julius was their emperor, they were forced to laugh out loud. It was the rules. If they kept a straight face or sulked or complained, he would throw them into prison until they cheered up.

Julius was making himself very unpopular – not just at home but throughout the empire and beyond.

The Queen of Spain refused to speak to him since he put a fake asp under her pillow. The King of France turned down all his invitations since Julius stuck a note to his back saying 'Kick me'. None of the senators would come to his birthday party – not after the last one when the cake exploded. His wife had left him and even his daughter disowned him and refused to let him come to her wedding.

Julius felt lonely. The only person who found him the slightest bit entertaining was his little grandson, Hilarious Giza. He decided to make young Hilarious his guest of honour at a spectacular show he had arranged at the coliseum.

The little lad was really looking forward to it. His grandad had promised him a seat in the front row. The programme looked very exciting. There was going to be a special race where the chariots were pulled by ostriches. There would be a mock sea battle with real ships and, best of all, there would be a gladiator fight.

Julius had been planning it for ages. He spent a fortune shipping wild beasts over from Africa, including a gorilla, a hippopotamus, some elephants and a herd of giraffes. He got a pack of wolves from India, a crate of cobras, several bears and more crocodiles than he could afford. He even ordered some marine creatures.

When the animals arrived, Julius housed them in the cells and passageways below the coliseum. Down there among the strings, pulleys and lifts that would bring the animals into the arena, he thought of all the brilliant jokes he could play on his audience.

Having arranged the animals, he hired musicians, magicians and dancing girls. He found the best caterer in town and ordered a load of honey cakes and five hundred barrels of olives. Once the food was sorted, Julius arranged for a team of plumbers to flood part of the arena. A warship was anchored at

each end. They were facing each other and ready to do battle.

Word soon got around. This was going to be the greatest show on Earth. Even though he was hated by most of his friends and family, Julius Teaser knew that the people of Rome would not be able to resist such a magnificent occasion, and he wasn't wrong.

The big day arrived and every one of the fifty thousand seats was taken. And right at the front, in the best seats overhanging the stage, sat Julius and his grandson.

'This is brilliant, Grandad!' said Hilarious Giza excitedly as the trumpeter came on to announce the first act.

'Wait until he tries to toot that trumpet,' said Julius. The trumpeter blew until his cheeks were puffed out like a hamster, but he couldn't get a single note out of his instrument. He felt inside the end and screamed as his hand struck something prickly.

'I stuffed a hedgehog up it!' said Julius.

'Oh, Grandad, you do the funniest things!' laughed Hilarious.

But that was just the beginning. Julius was up to his old tricks again and had thrown in some new ones. He put olive oil on the soles of the acrobats' slippers, so they could hardly stand up. He swapped the magic props so the magician accidentally sawed himself in half and he put bangers in the fire-eater's torch.

'Ha ha! I wish I'd thought of that, Grandad,' said Hilarious.

'You ain't seen nothing yet,' chortled Julius. It was time for the mock sea battle. This event was always very popular, but this time it came with a twist. Having loaded both ships with slaves, Julius Teaser had instructed them to ram 'the enemy' as hard as they could. What he hadn't told them was that he'd deliberately made holes in the bottom of both vessels and filled the water with man-eating sharks, fierce hippopotamuses and deadly jellyfish. The audience went wild.

'I knew it would be a crowd pleaser,' said Julius as the ships slowly sank, the sailors screamed and the water turned red. The audience clapped and cheered and for a moment, Julius felt certain that he had won back the hearts of the people.

'They love you, Grandad!' said Hilarious. But then, the tide turned. The honey cakes were handed round, but they weren't normal honey cakes – where was the fun in that? They were full of hot pepper, and the Patricians were gasping and choking and begging for water. The Plebeians thought this was great as they liked to see the rich folk suffering for once, but as soon as they bit into the olives, their mood changed; the olives were stuffed with dead flies.

'Why is nobody laughing except us, Grandad?' said Hilarious.

'You can't please all of the people all of the time,' smiled Julius. 'They will split their sides after the interval when they see what I've done to the gladiator.'

'Will the gladiator be fighting a lion?' asked Hilarious.

'No, an enormous man-eating tiger,' said Julius, snickering as a live skunk was catapulted into the cheap seats. 'Do you need the lavatorium, Hilarious? I need to go.'

Hilarious shook his head.

'I'll just sit here quietly and behave until you get back,' he said.

Julius Teaser left. And while he was gone, Hilarious did sit quietly, but he didn't behave. Not at all. He had been waiting for this moment for some time. He reached inside his toga and in two split seconds, the deed was done. He had placed an upturned pin on the Emperor's chair.

The crowd were getting bored, so the gladiator went into the ring slightly early and was strutting up and down, flexing his biceps and wooing the crowd, his sword still sheathed. There was a low terrifying growl and the crowd gasped as a massive tiger rose up through the floor on a plinth, pawing the air. The gladiator whisked round and held up his shield.

'Hurry up, Grandad!' yelled Hilarious. 'It's started. You'll miss the best bit.'

Julius Teaser rushed back to his seat, sat down, leapt up with a piercing shriek and fell backwards over the balcony into the arena below. He had fallen for the oldest trick in the book.

'It's behind you!' whooped the crowd. Julius turned in horror. Seeing that the tiger was about to pounce on him, he appealed to the gladiator, who had never forgotten the time Julius had loosened the buckle on his loincloth and it had fallen off in the middle of a fight.

'Defend me!' cried the Emperor. The gladiator pulled out his sword. To his surprise, it felt strangely light and as the tiger leapt, he realized what had happened – some joker had swapped his real weapon for a cardboard one.

'Nice one!' hooted Hilarious, certain that his grandad saw the funny side. We'll never know. As Julius Teaser was eaten alive, they say that somebody roared with laughter. But it was probably the tiger.

Percy Bysshe Smelley: Historical Background

The unlucky poet in this story gets his name from one of the most famous poets of the nineteenth century – Percy Bysshe Shelley. However, their names are about the only thing they have in common, because the real Percy Shelley came from a rich and powerful family and lived a wild and romantic life.

Shelley's father was a member of parliament, and the young Shelley was expected to follow his father into politics. However, Shelley had other things in mind. He was a rebel from a very young age – in fact, he got expelled from Oxford University for writing a shocking pamphlet about atheism. At the age of just nineteen, he ran away to Scotland with Harriet Westbrook, who was sixteen. He married Harriet, despite his father's disapproval (Harriet's father was an innkeeper and Shelley's father was furious that Shelley wanted to marry someone from a poorer family).

Harriet and Shelley had two children, but

unfortunately their marriage didn't last long. In 1814, when he was 22, Shelley met and fell in love with Mary Godwin. Mary was a writer herself, and went on to write *Frankenstein*. In 1816, Mary and Shelley were married. In 1818 they moved to Italy, where Mary became ill and two of the couple's children died. Despite all the sadness and difficulties, Percy Shelley continued to write. He produced some of his most famous poems during this period, including 'Prometheus Unbound' and 'Adonais'. On 8 July 1822, just before his 30th birthday, Percy Shelley died in a sailing accident. He is still remembered as one of the most important poets of his time.

Smelly London life in the nineteenth century

The Percy Smelley in the story lived a very different kind of life from Shelley. If you could magically transport yourself back in time to Percy's London in 1820, you would be amazed at the sights, sounds and smells all around you. The street sweepers constantly struggled to keep the roads free of horse manure – a big problem in a city full of horse-drawn carriages, carts and wagons. The air was grey from the hundreds and thousands of chimneys billowing with black coal smoke, and every surface was black and grimy with coal dust. Raw sewage ran through some of the gutters and down into the river Thames. The pavements were thronging with street sellers shouting about their wares – everything from apples and oranges to flowers, ribbons, fish and meat.

Did you know?

- Street sellers in London were often known as 'costermongers', which literally means 'apple sellers'. 'Coster' comes from 'costard', an old word for a type of apple.

- In 1850, a survey was made of the traffic around London Bridge. It found that 1,000 horse-drawn vehicles per hour passed through the area. More than 1,000 horses per hour ... that's a lot of manure. No wonder the street sweepers struggled to keep up!

Percy Bysshe Smelley: The Least Romantic Poet

What do you want to be when you grow up? You have lots of brilliant jobs to choose from. You could be anything from an astronaut to a zoologist. You could earn heaps of money and buy a big house and a flashy car. Or dedicate yourself to helping others.

Or you could be a poet. Don't snort, there are lots of good things about being a poet. You can work from home. Or at your nan's. Or in the bath. Wherever you feel most comfortable.

If it's a nice spring day, you can wander lonely as a cloud through a host of golden daffodils, like the famous poet William Wordsworth. If anyone asks what you're up to – such as a dog walker or a policeman – just explain that although it may look like you're just sitting in the park behind the tennis courts eating chips, actually you are working. You're writing poetry. It's your job.

There are other benefits. Unlike people in most professions, poets don't have to get up early. Pity the milkman up at the crack of dawn or the civil servant hurrying through the rush hour to make his breakfast meeting. Their lives are not their own.

But poets? They never have to watch the clock or explain to the boss why they are late. They are their own boss. They don't have to get up at all unless they need the toilet. Imagine malingering under the duvet all day and if your mother asks why you are being so lazy, simply point to your laptop and say, 'It may look as if I'm lying here idly, surrounded by bits of old pizza, but don't be fooled. What I'm really doing is working. I am writing verses in my head and waiting for my muse to arrive. It is not my fault if she is late.'

But being a poet isn't all good, and it never was. Creatively, you may spend years in torment trying to find the perfect line to finish your sonnet. Or struggle to find a word that rhymes with 'orange', only to find that there isn't one.

The money is terrible. You will have to beg, steal or borrow from family and friends or you will starve. If you manage to publish your work, you could be thrown into gaol like Oscar Wilde, just for saying the wrong thing and hanging out with the wrong friends.

Even worse, nobody will realize what a genius you are until after your death.

So what drives a person to be a poet, if not fame and fortune? If you study the poets of the past, the same reason keeps cropping up: good poetry makes you popular with the opposite sex. In Victorian times, romantic poems were all the rage. The poets were the rock stars of their day, flouncing around in their ruffly blouses and tight velvet trousers and being all sensitive. And that was just the men. Lord Byron only had to dip his quill in his ink and the ladies would swoon at his feet.

Poets were celebrities. They had fan clubs. They went on tour and hung out in the best clubs with their wacky mates. They were so cool that lots of teenage wannabes wanted that lifestyle and tried to knock out a few verses in the hope of becoming a star. But just like today, it was no good unless they had the X factor. And nobody had it less than Percy Bysshe Smelley.

Born in 1822 under a fishmonger's stall in Billingsgate Market, Percy never stood a chance with the girls. His mother named him after her teenage heart-throb, the poet Percy Bysshe Shelley, who'd had a hit with a catchy little poem called 'Ozymandias', but he hardly lived up to his name.

While Shelley's father was a politician, Percy's dad was in the poorhouse. While Shelley was handsome and fragrant, Percy looked like a pollock and stank of sardines.

But he had fine feelings and when he was sixteen he fell in love with a beautiful Irish flower girl called Gladdy O'Lee. Plucking up his courage, he wiped his fishy hands on his smelly apron and, running a quick comb through his nits, he went and asked her out.

'Why would I be courting an *eejit* like you?' she said, 'I want to marry one of those fine poetry men with all their pretty words and all.'

'I take it that's a no, then?' said Percy. He was disappointed, but he was so desperate to win her hand that he decided to give the poetry lark a go. There was only one problem. He couldn't read or write, and nor could his mother. Education was for rich kids. The only place Percy could get an education was at The Urchin School for Losers, where the masters were cruel and beat the pupils with birch twigs.

He didn't care. He was so in love with Gladdy that he decided she was worth the pain. The next day, he played truant from the fish stall and went into the classroom. He was a quick learner and after several thrashings, he soon got to grips with the Three R's – reading, writing and robbing – and came home with his first poem, 'Ode to Gladdy O'Lee'.

He showed it proudly to his mother who was busy cooking an old leather shoe over a candle for tea.

'What are all them squiggly lines on that slate?' she said.

'It's writing, Ma,' said Percy. 'Like what them posh kids do.'

Unfortunately, he never got to read it aloud.

'I ain't having none of that fancy writing in my slum!' she screeched. 'Fine words feed no brats. Go and gut some cod and earn yerself a proper livin'!'

Percy's mother often earned a few extra farthings as a bare-knuckle fighter, so he didn't like to argue. He carried on with his day job on the fish stall, but every evening he sat in the bed he shared with his with fifteen brothers and sisters, penning a poem for his beloved.

It wasn't easy. The bed was so crowded, he had hardly any room to move his writing elbow, and as he couldn't afford paper or ink, he had to write it in gravy on his pillowcase. Any mistakes were rubbed out with a lump of mutton fat – and there were a lot of mistakes – but after a final polish he was pleased with

it. He dressed in his best Sunday rags and went to read it to Gladdy O'Lee. She was sitting daintily on the pavement with a basket full of posies.

'Sweet violets!' she cried. 'Buy my violets. Penny a bunch!'

Percy Byshe Smelly whipped out his pillowcase.

'I don't have a penny, but I do have a poem for you!' he announced. 'It's called 'Ode to Gladdy O'Lee'.

'Let's hear it then', she said. He took a deep breath and began ...

'*Ode to Gladdy O'Lee*
My love has the eyes of a cod fish.
My love has the lips of a trout.
Her hair, it reminds me of seaweed.
Sweetheart, can I take you out?'

49

Gladdy listened in horror, but as Percy didn't know much about girls he thought she was impressed . He cleared his throat and read the second verse.

'I'll give you a pint of my winkles.
I'll give you some cockles for free.
I've got wonderful mussels, my darling.
I love you. Oh, please marry me!'

To his surprise, Gladdy burst into tears. At first he was pleased. She had obviously found his poem very moving.

'It's from the heart,' he said. 'I meant every word.'

'I hate you!' she said, 'Your poem stinks. You can keep your *shellfish* remarks.' With that, she whacked Percy Byshe Smelley round the head with her flower basket and everything went black.

When he woke up on the kerb he thought he was dreaming. He was lying in the arms of an angel. It was an angel with a ruddy face and big biceps, wearing a blood-stained apron, but she had a kind smile and a sweet voice.

'I fink that *pome,* what you wrote, was luvverly,' she said. Percy rubbed his eyes. It was Beryl, the butcher's daughter. He'd known her for years, but it was the first time he'd ever noticed her properly. She was gazing into his black eye.

'If you writ me luvverly words such as them, I would marry you,' said Beryl. Percy gazed back.

'Really?' he said, 'Can I borrow your pencil?' She took it from behind her ear, wiped the mince off and handed it to him.

'I will bring you a poem tomorrow,' he said. Beryl fluttered her eyelashes.

'Meet me outside the knackers yard at noon,' she said.

Percy ran home across the cobbled streets. This was his big chance to get a girlfriend. He had to write the best poem ever. He went upstairs, threw himself onto the bed and thought of Beryl, hoping that inspiration would come.

After a sleepless night trying to find a word that rhymed with kidney, the poem finally came together in the early hours of dawn. As he'd run out of pillow cases, he had to write it on a dirty hanky but at least the poem was clean and well-composed. Even so, would Beryl like it? Percy's last poem had gone down so badly with Gladdy O'Lee, he'd lost all confidence in himself as a poet.

'Oh well. Faint heart never won fair maiden,' he muttered. He got out of his nightshirt, slipped into his smartest fish overalls and set off to find the future Mrs Smelley with his poem in his pocket.

What if she stands me up? he thought. He needn't have worried. As he dashed into the knackers yard,

Beryl was waiting for him.

'Let's hear it, handsome,' she said. 'I'm all ears.' Percy had never noticed her ears before and now she'd come to mention it, they were large, but that was a good thing. The bigger the ears, the better she would hear his poem. He pulled the hanky out, gave it a shake and began to read.

'*Ode to Beryl Brisket*
My love is as sweet as pan-fried veal.
Her hands are as soft as a jellied eel.
Her heart is as tender as shoulder of lamb.
Cooked in a bucket of redcurrant jam.'

He paused for a second, nervous in case Beryl didn't like it. Being hit round the head by a flower girl's basket was one thing, being slayed by a butcher's axe was quite another.

'Is that it?' said Beryl. 'Only you writ Miss Gladdy two verses and she's no better than she should be and ain't half so loving and grateful as what I is.'

Encouraged by the fact that she wanted to hear another verse, Percy continued.

'Beryl oh Beryl, I'm all of a quiver.
I love you right down to your kidneys and liver.
You may be as tough as old braising steak
But marry me now or my heart will break.'

He fell on to one knee and produced a ring. It used to belong to his grandmother who had stolen it from a rich lady. By now, a large crowd had gathered – the butcher, the baker and the candlestick maker, not to mention the costermonger, the iron monger, the organ grinder, his monkey, a gang of pick-pockets and a mudlark.

'Garn, marry him!' said the Butcher. 'Better to be a fishwife than an old maid.'

'I will not be a fishwife!' cried Beryl.

The crowd fell silent, apart from the sound of Percy's sobs, certain that he'd been rejected. He was wrong. Beryl hadn't finished with him yet.

'But I will be a poet's wife!' she exclaimed, 'Percy Smelley, that was the most romantic poem I ever did hear in all my days. I will marry you!' Percy dried his eyes on his own poem and they fell into each other's arms.

'That's my girl!' said the butcher, 'Let's have a right ol' cockney knees-up.'

'Hurrah!' whooped the crowd.

So they rolled out the barrel, they all had a barrel of fun and Percy married his *sole* mate. And the moral of the story? Never pooh-pooh the power of poetry.

It's a whole lot stronger than aftershave.

The Wrong Brothers: Historical Background

The Wright brothers, Orville and Wilbur, are famous as the main inventors of the aeroplane. The Wrong brothers, on the other hand, never did anything useful. It's not really their fault though – they could hardly invent the aeroplane if they didn't even exist!

An inventive childhood

Wilbur Wright was born in 1867 in Indiana, in the USA. His brother Orville was born four years later and together the Wrights went on to form an unstoppable inventing team.

Their father, Milton Wright, was a church minister, and often had to travel on business for the church. When he went away, he usually brought back something interesting for his children. After one trip, he presented the boys with an amazing spinner, a bit like a helicopter. It was powered by an elastic band and to Orville and Wilbur's delight, it actually flew! This gift of a toy helicopter seems to have triggered the boys' interest in studying and building flying machines. They were mechanically-minded and enjoyed making and designing all kinds of machines, not just flying ones.

The Wright Brothers in partnership

When they left school, Wilbur and Orville decided to open a printing business together. They actually built their own printing press, using an old tombstone and some spare parts! At around this time, they also became interested in bicycles. They started off repairing bicycles for their friends and this gradually grew into a business. Some people think that working with bicycles (which are often wobbly to ride at first) helped the Wrights to work out how to make their aeroplanes stable during flight.

Taking off

In the late 1890s, the Wrights started to work seriously on the idea of flight. Wilbur wrote off to the Smithsonian, an important American scientific institution, to get all of the information he could about the subject. It didn't take him long to read everything they sent and the brothers quickly started work on their own theories. They tested their ideas using kites, and in 1900 they built their own glider. Following a test flight at Kitty Hawk in North Carolina, the brothers created a new and better glider with a wingspan of nearly seven metres. Their new, improved glider crashed, so they built their own wind tunnel to research the effects of wind on different wing shapes. Their next glider was a great success, gliding nearly 189 metres.

Airborne!

Having made a successful glider, the Wrights then started designing a flying machine. They had to design and make their own propellers and engine from scratch, since the engines used in other machines were too heavy to go into a flying machine. Their first aeroplane, the Flyer, eventually made the world's first manned flight on 17 December 1903. The flight lasted twelve seconds, covering a massive 36.5 metres! However, the brothers were not downhearted. They started working on improvements and in 1905 they managed to perfect their design. The aeroplane age had begun!

Did you know?

- Wilbur Wright was brilliant at school, but Orville was possibly a little bit more like the Wrong Brothers in the story. He was an average student, well known for his mischievous behaviour. He left school early to start the printing business.

- The brothers chose Kitty Hawk as a good place to test their gliders because it had very strong winds and some big sandy dunes which would be useful if (and when) the gliders crashed!

The Wrong Brothers:
The World's Worst Pilots

For as long as humans have walked the Earth, they have wished they could fly.

Many have tried and failed. In Greek mythology, Daedalus thought he'd cracked it. Having studied the birds, he made wings out of wax and feathers for himself and his son Icarus. Flapping their arms like mad geese, Daedalus and Icarus took to the sky. Sadly, Icarus' high hopes of soaring like an eagle were dashed – he flew too close to the sun, his wings melted and he plummeted like a penguin.

Aerodynamics has come a long way since then – over eighteen million plane journeys are taken every year. But we might never have got off the ground if it hadn't been for the Wright Brothers. And the Wrong Brothers, of course.

At the end of the nineteenth century, both sets of brothers went to the same school in Ohio. But while Wilbur and Orville Wright were good boys, Butch and Buster Wrong were quite the opposite.

Since reception class, the Wrong Brothers had bullied the Wrights. It was Butch who dropped a toad down Wilbur's shorts in P.E. It was Buster who put a worm in Orville's cheese sandwich. And both of them put baby skunks in the Wright boys' satchels.

The Wrongs never got caught. The Wright Brothers never told the teacher or stood up to them – not because they were wimps but because their dad was a minister and they knew it was wrong to grass the other kids up.

It all came to a head when the class was given a project to do over the holidays. They had to make a model of a flying machine – anything from a kite to a glider – and there would be a prize for the pupil who flew it the furthest on the school field.

'Homework in the holidays?' groaned Butch. 'Not fair!'

'How exciting!' squealed Wilbur. 'Imagine, Orville! When we grow up, we might even invent a machine heavier than air that people can fly in.'

'Dream on,' snorted Buster. 'And I suppose one day, men will land on the moon!' Oh, how the rest of the class laughed.

Wilbur and Orville couldn't wait to start. They went to Papa's library, looked in his history books and did their research. There was a fascinating chapter about the Ancient Chinese, who had invented the flying paper lantern.

'All we need is a paper bag and an oil lamp,' said Wilbur. 'It says here that hot air will cause the balloon to rise.'

'I'll fetch some matches,' said Orville.

That afternoon, they carried their model proudly down the garden path and, setting light to the oil, they watched in amazement as the balloon rose into the air and disappeared over the fence.

'Oh criminy! It's drifting into the Wrongs' garden!' said Wilbur. 'I should have put a string on it.'

Buster and Butch looked up from playing, whipped out their catapults and fired. There was a loud pop.

'Good shot, Butch!' said Buster.

'Oh well. Back to the drawing board,' sighed Orville. The Wrights went back indoors and did some more swotting.

'The Wrong Brothers are bound to copy our balloon and say it was their idea,' said Wilbur. 'We will have to make something bigger and better.'

An interesting diagram had caught his eye – a wooden flying machine with four wings, invented by an Italian in 1648. He read the bumph.

'*Burattini's Flying Dragon*. It says here that it lifted a cat into the air.' Their eyes fell on their pet tabby, curled up on the rug.

'I'll fetch the wood and some screws,' said Orville. 'Meet me in the yard.'

'Here, Puss,' said Wilbur.

Lured by the sound of hammering and miaowing, the Wrong Brothers left their little sister tied to a totem pole and peered through a hole in the Wrights' fence. By now, they had finished making their model of the Flying Dragon and were busy strapping the cat into the pilot seat.

'That beats a balloon any day!' said Orville. 'It's nice and windy. Let's take it to the top of a hill for a test flight.'

'Good idea,' said Wilbur. 'Don't worry, Puss, it's only a small drop. I've made you this crash helmet out of an old tin mug.'

Off they went, pulling their latest invention to the nearest steep slope, little realizing that the

Wrong Brothers were secretly stalking them with their pet bulldog.

'Let's ambush them, holler like mad and scare them off,' whispered Buster.

'Then what?' said Butch.

'Then we'll steal their winged catmobile, pretend we made it and win the competition.'

But things didn't go to plan. As the Wrongs burst out of the bushes, waving tomahawks and yelling their war cry: 'Wah wah wah wah wah', the dog started barking. The cat panicked, leapt out of the cockpit with a strap still attached to its collar and dragged the whole contraption down the hill. At the bottom, the Flying Dragon hit a tree and flew no more.

'What a load of rubbish!' sneered the Wrong Brothers.

The Wright Brothers gazed sadly at their shattered machine but, never ones to bear a grudge, they soon pulled themselves together.

'Look on the bright side,' said Orville. 'At least Puss wasn't hurt.' They went back to their books. They had plenty of ideas, but none of them were practical.

'We could make a glider like Jean-Marie Le Bris,'

said Orville brightly. 'In 1856, he used a horse to pull it along a beach. It flew nearly two hundred yards.'

'Dang! We don't have a horse,' said Wilbur.

'Or a beach,' said Orville.

The end of the holidays was looming fast and the Wrights still hadn't finished their project. Meanwhile, there were rumours that the Wrongs had tied their little sister to a kite and let it go, and that she'd flown to Mexico. But it was only wishful thinking.

In the end – as so often happens when children get stuck with their homework – Orville and Wilbur's father came to the rescue. A Frenchman called Alphonse Penaud had successfully flown a model aircraft powered by twisted rubber in Paris, and seeing a little model of the same plane in a toy shop, Mr Wright bought one for his sons.

The timing was perfect. Copying the basic design but adding their own twist to the wings, the boys launched their own model indoors. They kept the curtains shut so the Wrong Brothers couldn't snoop. As they observed the way the toy aircraft swept the ornaments off the mantelpiece, they modified it a bit.

And then a bit more. By tea time, it flew far better; straight through the front room, twice round the kitchen and right along the hall.

'If we don't win the competition now, I'm a spaceman,' said Orville.

'Where are all my rubber bands?' said Mrs Wright. 'I'm sure I had a full packet.'

It was the first day of the autumn term and all the children arrived back at school with their projects under their arms – except for Buster and Butch. Bored with sabotaging the Wright Brothers' early flying machines, they'd spent a wonderful summer rustling cattle, which left no time to complete their project.

'I sure hope we won't get detention,' said Butch.

'We won't,' said Buster, 'because look who's a-comin' round the corner.' It was Orville and Wilbur, carrying a cake tin. The Wrong brothers blocked their path.

'What's in that tin, boy?' said Butch.

'It's ... blueberry pie,' said Wilbur. He was a good lad, but a bad liar. Buster was on to him and snatched the tin.

'My, I sure do like blueberry pie!' he said. 'I'll have me a slice of that.' He flipped the lid off the tin. The little plane powered by elastic bands was inside it.

'Why, that ain't no finger-lickin' pie!' said Butch, 'I do believe it's my entry for the class competition.'

'It sure is!' said Buster.

'But it's ours!' said Orville, 'Give it back, please. That's stealing.'

'Giddy up, ol' buddy!' grinned Butch, pushing Orville out of the way. 'Me and my brother? We got us a competition to win!'

It goes without saying that the nasty Wrong Brothers won first prize with the model that they had stolen from the Wrights. And although Orville and Wilbur never forgot the humiliation of being put in detention for 'not handing in their project', they grew up to be well-adjusted young men.

They never lost their fascination for flying. Following their dream of designing a plane with an engine that could carry passengers, they built a series of kites and gliders based on the experiments of the men who'd tried before them.

While the Wrights were busy fine-tuning their calculations, the notorious Wrong Brothers reared their ugly heads again. Having escaped the hangman's noose, they went on the run and were camping in Kill Devil Hills when something shot overhead and startled them out of their sleeping bags. It was Orville, cruising in his new glider, Flyer 1.

'Holy Smoke! Those Wright boys done took that school project too far this time,' muttered Buster.

'Shall we take 'em down a peg or two?' said Butch. 'For ol' times' sake?' Orville flew an awesome 120 feet, landed and let his brother have a go.

'Sure we will,' said Buster, suddenly noticing a small crowd which had gathered to watch the glider. 'Keep your head down, Butch. There are three bounty hunters, a showgirl and a gold digger taking photos.'

The Wrong Brothers hid, but later that day they saw Wilbur flying even further than his brother – 852 feet in 59 seconds.

'Heck! Those darn Wrights is gonna find fame and fortune in the field of aviation,' sulked Butch. 'I want a piece of that, don't you, Buster? Can we steal their flying machine again and say it's ours?'

Buster shook his head. 'No, siree. Too many witnesses. This time, we're gonna take 'em down good.'

As the months went by, the Wrong Brothers spied on the Wrights, who had built a wind tunnel full of clever devices to measure the drag and lift on over two hundred wing designs.

'How come I never got no wind tunnel for Christmas?' sulked Butch. 'Shall I get me a big stick of dynamite and blow it up when nobody's looking?'

'I got me a much better idea,' whispered Buster. 'One where nobody can pin the blame on us.'

'Tell me, tell me, tell me!' said Butch excitedly. Buster nodded mysteriously.

'All in good time, buddy.'

Butch didn't have to wait too long. In the summer of 1905, the Wrong Brothers disguised themselves as trees, stood on Huffman Prairie and waited for the Wrights to arrive with their latest flying machine.

'Hot diggity! Look at the wings on that!' said Butch. Buster put his finger to his lips.

'Hush your mouth, boy. You're meant to be a tree.' They watched as Wilbur climbed into the cockpit.

'Chocks away!' he whooped to Orville. The glider taxied along the grass, gathered speed – faster and faster – then it lifted into the air.

'What I don't get,' said Butch, 'is how something so heavy stays up in the sky.'

'Maybe it won't,' grinned Buster. 'What goes up must come down.' Butch looked at him and smiled.

'Have you done filled the fuel tank with sugar?' Buster shook his head.

'Those boys are way too ambitious,' he whispered. 'I got a feeling they gonna smash up Flyer 3 all by their own selves.'

Whether he was psychic or psycho, his prediction came true; the new glider went wildly out of control and crashed. To the Wrong Brothers' disappointment, Wilbur survived, but he was battered and bruised. Orville limped the broken plane back to the wind tunnel and took his brother home to patch him up. He wouldn't be flying anywhere for a while.

'Dang! He wasn't deaded,' sighed Butch, slipping out of his tree costume.

'Next time,' said Buster. 'I have a cunnin' plan, remember?'

When the coast was clear, Butch followed his brother to the wind tunnel where Flyer 3 lay in bits. He watched as Buster grabbed a pot of glue and a saw and gave the glider a make-over.

'Why are you a-fixing it for them?' said Butch. 'Why are you making the wings so darn big? How come you shifted the elevator? That bit don't go there.'

'I aint fixin' it, I'm a-meddling,' said Buster, screwing the rudder on a separate handle. 'This baby is gonna go up-diddly-up-up and go down-diddly-down-down! Pass me that monkey wrench.'

'Won't they notice it's all switched around?' said Butch. Buster tapped his nose.

'I'll post a letter to Wilbur pretending to be Orville, saying he's fixed Flyer 3 up good, as a nice surprise. That boy will never doubt his own brother.'

'And his plane will go down-diddly-down-down?' said Butch.

'Ohhh yeah.'

The fatal day came. Or so they hoped. As soon as Wilbur was fit to fly, he hurried to the wind tunnel to see what a grand job Orville had done on Flyer 3. He was a little surprised by the changes Orville had made but, trusting his brother completely, he jumped into the cockpit and hurtled off down the runway.

'Oh happy day!' said Buster as the glider lifted into the air. 'I sure do like a funeral.' But to the Wrongs' dismay, the glider stayed up. It stayed up for 39 minutes and 23 seconds, flew 24 miles and landed perfectly.

'You fixed it too good, Buster!' yelled Butch. It was true. By sheer fluke, the Wrong Brothers' fiendish fiddling had created the perfect flying machine. But they got no thanks for it. The Wrights took all the praise. Wilbur went down in history as the first man to fly a plane under full control and land it back safely.

Which just goes to show that two Wrongs don't make a Wright.

WRIGHT BROTHERS' FLYER

Marco Pillow:
Historical Background

Marco Polo was a famous traveller and writer who lived over 700 years ago. He was one of the first Europeans to visit China and became famous because of the stories he told about his travels. But were the stories true, or were they (like the story of Marco Pillow that follows) a pack of lies?

Marco Polo's early life

Marco was born in Venice, Italy in about 1254. He came from a rich family – both his father Niccolo and his uncle Maffeo were successful jewel merchants. When Marco was a child, his father and uncle went on a trip to Asia and visited the court of Kublai Khan, the Mongol ruler of China. Kublai Khan was interested in finding out more about Christianity, so he asked the Polos to persuade the Pope to send some scholars on a special mission to explain Christianity to him.

The Polos duly went back to Europe to arrange this. In 1271, they headed back to China again with two missionaries from the Pope, taking the young Marco with them.

A long stay in China

It is a long way from Venice to China and unfortunately for Marco, the Wright brothers weren't around yet. So the journey alone took Marco, Niccolo and Maffeo four years. They then spent the following seventeen years in China. We don't know very much for certain about those years, but Marco must have impressed Kublai Khan because he was sent on several official trips around China, which gave him the opportunity to get to know different parts of the country.

In about 1292, the Polos had the chance to make a trip to Persia (Iran), accompanying a Mongol princess who was going to marry the Persian ruler. On the way to Iran, they visited Sumatra and India, then they travelled home to Venice again via Constantinople.

Marco in jail

Not long after arriving back in Venice, Marco Polo became involved in a war between Venice and Genoa. He was captured and imprisoned by the Genoese. His cell mate was a writer from Pisa called Rustichello. Rustichello was intrigued by the stories Marco told about his travels and started to write them down. Rustichello's finished book certainly made an exciting read. *The Travels of Marco Polo* became extremely popular and was translated into many languages, making Marco famous.

After Marco Polo was released from prison in about 1299, he became a merchant like his father and uncle before him. He married and had three children – but none of them was called Marco Pillow! Marco Polo died in 1324 and was buried at the church of San Lorenzo in Venice.

Were Marco's stories true?

Experts are still arguing about how much of Marco Polo's account of his adventures was true. It is hard to be certain because, after the Mongols stopped ruling China, the Ming dynasty took over and they did not welcome Western travellers. So, for a long time, it was very hard for Europeans to go to China and verify Marco's stories. However, nowadays many experts believe that Marco Polo's description of China is at least broadly true.

Did you know?

- Marco Polo's stories inspired lots of later travellers – including the famous explorer Christopher Columbus.

- In Italy, *The Travels of Marco Polo* was known as *Il Milione*, or *The Million*. Nowadays no one is quite sure how the book got this strange title. It might be because in the Middle Ages, many people thought the book was full of 'a million lies'.

Marco Pillow: The World's Laziest Explorer

Hands up if you were born in Venice in the thirteenth century. If so, you might have bumped into a very famous man with a beard. No, not Father Christmas. Guess again. If you said Marco Polo, go to the top of the class and have a gold star.

Ah, but what was he famous for? With a surname like Polo, you would be forgiven for thinking he invented mints with holes in, but he didn't. They were invented 700 years later by a bloke called Bargewell who worked in a sweet factory and was clearly bored.

Marco Polo did something far more exciting for a living. His daddy was a rich merchant who traded in the Middle East. In between trips, Daddy often talked shop to little Marco, who picked up lots of tips about buying and selling things abroad, how to count foreign money and how to handle cargo ships.

When he was seventeen, he didn't sit around

playing computer games all day – they hadn't been invented yet, and nor had teenagers. Instead, he went on a gap year to Asia with his dad and his uncle Maffeo.

Some gap year! Marco had so much fun visiting China, India and Japan that he stayed there for twenty-four years. All in all, he travelled about 15,000 old-fashioned miles and, bearing in mind that the car didn't exist, that was an amazing feat on amazing feet.

The Travels of
Marco Polo

At the ripe old age of forty-one, Marco decided to go home and show everyone his manly beard, but that didn't happen. Shock horror – Venice was at war with Genoa and he was captured and taken prisoner.

In prison, Marco made friends with an inmate called Rustichello. Rusticello, who had a name like a large stringed instrument left out in the rain, owned a pencil. Night after night, Marco amused his cell mate with tales about his crazy holiday and Rusti wrote it all down, adding a few random stories of his own for good measure.

The book was called *The Travels of Marco Polo*. It wasn't a great title but it was a very good read and soon became a best seller in the West. Until then, nobody in Europe had been much further than the bottom of their road (and they were the adventurous ones, as some didn't even have roads). There were no package holidays. They couldn't just turn up at the airport and catch a flight, so they had no idea what was going on in the Far East – it was too far.

Until Marco put everyone in the picture with his tantalizing tales, no one knew what Asian people looked like, how they lived or what they'd invented.

It was a bit like finding out that fairies really existed, and a lot of Marco's readers thought he was making it all up.

'The Chinese use money made out of paper?' they hooted. 'Are you nuts? It would tear! They burn black lumps called coal to cook their food? Marco, you are having a laugh.'

Happily, he managed to persuade a lady called Donata Badoer that it was all true and that he was the greatest explorer ever. She married him – which had nothing to do with the fact that he was loaded – and gave birth to three girls: Fantina, Bellela and Moreta.

What nobody tells you is that Mr and Mrs Polo also had a son. They didn't like to talk about him and this is why ...

It was Daddy Marco's greatest wish that when Baby Marco grew up, he would follow in his father's footsteps. Marco Senior wanted his son to go back to the Far East and prove that *The Travels of Marco Polo* were not a load of old bunkum.

However, Baby Marco was nothing like his dad. He was the laziest kid ever. All he wanted to do was lie in his cot and cuddle his pillow.

'Has he no sense of adventure!' wailed Mr Polo.

'Give him a chance,' said Mrs Polo. 'He's only three months old.' But things didn't improve. As he grew, Little Marco had no interest in going anywhere except back to bed.

'I can't understand it!' said Mr Polo, 'He has no concept of foreign affairs, even though I read him *The Travels of Marco Polo* every bedtime.'

'He's three, dear,' said Mrs Polo. 'He's only just going to nursery school.' Big Marco wasn't impressed.

'I didn't get where I am today by going to nursery school!' he raged. 'I went all the way to Asia! Did I ever tell you about the time I had lunch with the Chinese Emperor … ?'

'Yes, yes,' sighed his wife. 'Several times. Shush, you'll wake Little Marco.'

By the time he was seventeen, Little Marco was a lot larger, mostly because he hardly moved. If he did bother to travel any distance – to the toilet or the kitchen – he always took his pillow in case he needed a nap, which is how he got his nickname.

'Marco Pillow!' said his father. 'Get up! I want you to go and discover the Great Wall of China.

I forgot to mention it in my memoirs. Now no one believes I went there, apart from your mother.'

'I won't go. I hate you!' said teenage Marco, and he went back to sleep. Mr Polo decided to take drastic action. He went down to the docks and paid some sailors to kidnap his son while he slept.

'Put him on a slow boat to China,' he said. 'And make sure he writes about his trip to prove that all those things I said about the Chinese are true. Did I ever tell you they actually burn stuff called "coal" to cook their ...'

'Several times,' groaned the sailors. 'Must dash. Got a boy to kidnap.'

Marco Pillow woke up in his jimjams aboard the *Nutty Shark* in the middle of the ocean. He thought he was having a nightmare and, clutching his pillow, he went up on deck.

'Hoist the main brace!' said the Captain. 'Swab the decks or you'll walk the plank.'

'*Walk*?' yawned Marco. 'Can't you give me a lift?' The Captain cracked his whip.

'Any more of your lip and I'll keelhaul you, Mr Pillow ... Mr Pillow?'

Marco had nodded off on the ship's wheel and was snoring. The furious Captain was so busy putting him in the scuppers with a hosepipe on him, he didn't notice that the wheel had been shifted during the scuffle or that the *Nutty Shark* had steered off-course.

'*Land ahoy*!' yelled the bosun. 'Drop anchor!' As they rowed towards the shore, Marco Pillow couldn't believe his eyes.

'Trees with hairy nuts!' he exclaimed. 'Huge grey beasts with big ears and dangly noses! Are you sure this is China? It's nothing like the flora and fauna in Dad's book.' The Captain gave him a horrible stare. No one had ever questioned his judgment before.

'Of course it's China ... *isn't* it, lads?'

The rest of the crew, including Mr Wong, the ship's cook, had a sneaking suspicion that it wasn't, but they didn't like to disagree with him in case they were flayed with the cat-o'-nine-tails.

'Aye aye, Captain!' they said.

Shielding his eyes from the glaring sun, the Captain took his men across the beach and through the jungle.

'Sharpen your pencil, Master Pillow,' he said. 'Start writing and sketching. Record every beast, bird and native custom. Your father has promised me a large bounty if you do.'

'Ugh. I hate coconut,' sulked Marco as he struggled to think of a title for his project.

'How about *My Trip to China*?' suggested the first mate.

'Genius,' said Marco, sucking his pencil wearily, as a giraffe wandered past.

'Monday,' he yawned as he did a little sketch. 'Today I saw an orange and brown checked beast with a really long neck ... does anyone know what it's called, guys?' Nobody did. After all, they'd never seen a giraffe before – there weren't any in Venice.

'We could ask that Chinese man hiding in the bushes with a blow dart,' suggested the bosun.

'I'm not convinced he's Chinese,' said Mr Wong. Marco thought about it for two seconds.

'I'm too tired to talk to him,' he said, plumping up his pillow. 'I'll just make up a silly name for the beast. Who's going to know?' But he couldn't think of one.

'How about *camelopard*?' said the first mate, who was desperate to go home to his wife and kids.

'Thanks, mate,' said Marco, scribbling it down. 'That's one page done. Phew, I'm exhausted.' As he curled up and closed his eyes, the first mate and second mate exchanged worried glances.

'If this kid keeps going to sleep, he'll never fill his notebook up,' said the first mate. 'Captain won't get his bounty till he does. We could be stuck here in China for years.'

'It's Africa,' whispered the second mate. 'You know that, I know that. Which begs the question: how is Pillow going to find the Great Wall of China if we're in the Congo?'

'He could pretend he's seen it,' said the first mate. 'He was happy enough to make things up like *camelopard.* He's a lazy cheat, he'll love the idea. Just don't tell him we're in Africa in case he blabs in front of his old man.' It seemed like a plan.

'But how do we fool the Captain?' said the second mate.

'He's not the sharpest cutlass in the cabin,' grinned the first. 'We'll find the nearest old wall we can and tell him it's the Great One.'

It was 100 degrees in the shade and the mosquitos were biting. Keen to get out of the jungle as soon as possible, the crafty crew members waited until the Captain was out of earshot, put a tree frog down Marco's shorts to wake him up and explained their labour-saving idea.

'Brilliant,' said Marco. 'So I can pad this notebook out with made-up animals and plants, along with any that wander past while I'm lying here?'

'Yep,' said the first mate.

'And I don't even have to find the real Great Wall of China because it could take years and Dad will never find out?'

'Yep.'

'In which case,' said Marco, 'do we have to find a wall at all? I could easily draw a big one from my imagination without having to get up. It would save a lot of walking.'

'Nope. We have to fool the Captain,' said the second mate. 'We won't need to go far. We'll be back aboard the *Nutty Shark* by teatime, me hearty.'

Ah, famous last words. Three days after they set off, there wasn't a wall in sight. There were some mud huts in the village, but even the Captain knew that you can't make a Great Wall out of mud.

They trekked on and on with Marco complaining every step of the way.

'Are we there yet, second mate?' he moaned. 'My feet hurt.'

'Nope. Draw that leathery thing over there with the horn on its nose. No, not the Captain! The Hipponoseros or whatever it's called.'

Five minutes later: 'Are we nearly there yet, second mate?'

'Nooooo! Just sketch that big pink bird. I wish I could flamin' go home too.'

Sunday 14th May 1317. Saw a Flamingo. scribbled Marco.

Meanwhile, the bosun was savaged by a man-eating lion, the second mate fell in quicksand and the Captain was delirious with malaria.

'Pink elephants. I'm seeing pink elephants!' he shrieked. 'I'm never coming back for all the tea in China.'

Just when Marco thought things couldn't get any worse, a hyena chewed his pillow. He couldn't sleep without it and he was tired, hungry and thirsty.

'China is pants!' he sulked. 'I can't think what dad saw in it.'

By now, his water bottle was empty. The vultures were hovering and as he crawled along, he suddenly spotted something sparkling in the distance.

'Tell me it's a wall!' said the second mate who was crawling along behind him. But it wasn't. It was a waterfall – the source of a river that no one had ever discovered before, but Marco didn't know that. He just wanted to fill up his water bottle, get back to the ship and go to sleep.

'You might as well draw that waterfall now we're here,' said the second mate. 'It might be of great historical importance.' Marco shook his head.

'No, I'm going to draw a great big wall and you can't stop me. If I'd done it in the first place instead of listening to you, I'd be home by now.'

He licked the end of his pencil, wrote *The Great Wall* and drew a pile of higgledy-piggeldy bricks beneath the title. Thus, Marco Pillow made his last entry in *My Trip To China* and snapped his notebook shut. Shortly afterwards, some wandering nomads guided him and what was left of the crew back to the *Nutty Shark* and they sailed back to Venice.

Sadly, there was nothing in young Marco Pillow's book to support the claim that Old Marco Polo's trip to the Far East was genuine. It only took one clever clogs to see the drawings, recognize the 'camelopard' and point out loudly that giraffes were only found in Africa.

This could only mean that the sketch of the Great Wall of China must have been made in the wrong country and was a fraud. Word spread and not only was Marco Senior wrongly accused of lying about where he'd been, Marco Junior was rightly accused of being a useless ninny with no sense of adventure.

Venice Daily

Explorers:
Liar and Ninny

It was a bit unfair. Four centuries later, the source of the Nile was finally discovered – but the truth is, Marco Pillow found it first. It was in the exact spot where he drew his Great Wall, but nobody knew that because he was too lazy to write it down. If only he'd drawn that waterfall, Marco Pillow would have been the most famous explorer ever born.

Remember that the next time you rush your homework.

About the author

I was born in St Albans and have been writing since I could chew a pencil. I had my first book published by Andersen Press in 1980 (*The Tale of Georgie Grub*) and have now written over 250 books for which I have won glittering prizes.

I've worked as a waitress, till girl and reptile vet's assistant. I've worked in advertising and have written lots of TV programmes for children. I got married at London Zoo as I'm very fond of animals and I write with a cat, rat or a rabbit on my lap.

I found history a bit boring at school, so I amused myself by inventing pretend historical characters and writing rude songs about them. When the opportunity came to write *Hysterical Historicals*, I leapt at it.